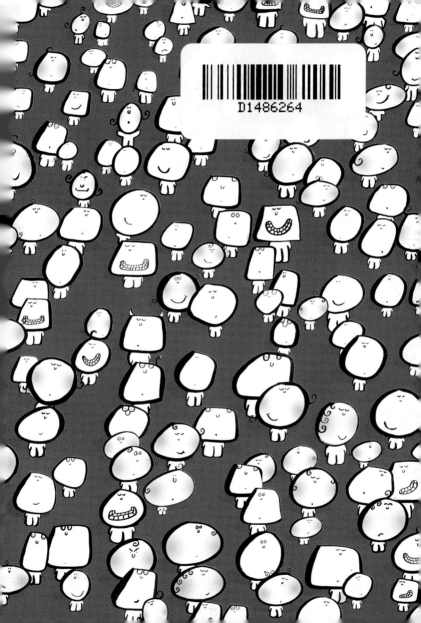

drink!

with Vimrod

drink!

Wine is made to be **drunk**,
I am drunk,
therefore
am **i** wine?

Vimrd by Lisa Swerling and Ralph Lazar

HarperCollins*Entertainment*
An Imprint of HarperCollins*Publishers*

if it
started to rain
champagne

would you:

1. call the police?
2. get one large bucket?
3. get two large buckets?
4. get three large buckets?
5. get four large buckets?

6. get as many **buckets**

as humanly possible?

is there more to life
than watching
sport on tv?

Yes!

watching sport on tv
with a beer

yesterday
i felt **blue**

so i had some **red** wine

now i feel

purple

je suis un
bottle of fine red wine.
you love me
and i, in turn, accept
the compliment and
am willing to be
ravished

the path of life is well-trodden

especially the section that leads to and from the **pub**

my favourite **food** is
anything that is washed
down by
wine

 YUM! YUM

i am on the cabinet

Minister of Beverage Affairs

(fortuitously the cabinet happens to be the liquor cabinet)

the **best** way to spend your time is by lying back on a huntershlossen with a glass of hummentassen while having your head gently scratched by a shtonkenellenbogen

(really, it works well)

if life is mount everest

you'll find me in the wine bar at base camp

whisky
focuses
the mind

can i have
another
plateful
please
?

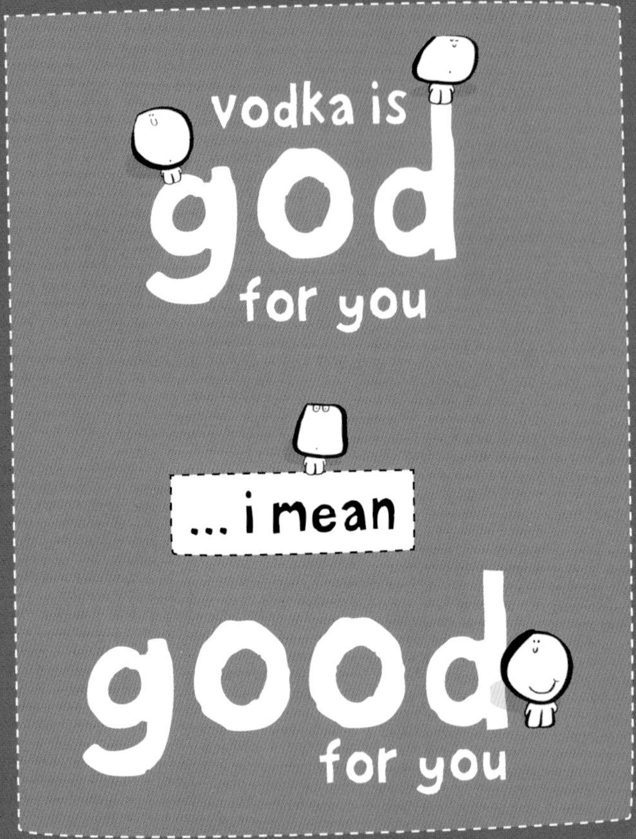
vodka is
god
for you
... i mean
good
for you

a man's body is built to chop down **trees** and *drink beer*

if there are no trees to chop down, it is fully within his rights to drink beer

all the time

deep, deep

inside the brain of every man is a tiny, tiny pub that serves a broad selection of lagers, stouts, ales, etc. plus some most excellent hot meals

the basic elements of life are genes, atoms and champagne

really, it has been proved by scientists and it was in the newspaper

i was abducted by ALIENS

i was really quite scared
but then they offered me some
little drinkies and i felt fine

the answer to the
big question is love

but the answer to all the little
questions is *good* red *wine*

nothing like a **cold**
beer on a *hot*
day

or on a
Cool
day

or
even on
a cold
day

all you
need is
LOVE,

and
gin,

GIN

and
tonic.

TONIC

lisa swerling + ralph lazar are two of the UK's most familiar graphic artists. Through their company Last Lemon they have spawned a catwalk of popular cartoon characters, which includes Harold's Planet, The Brainwaves, Blessthischick and, of course, Vimrod.

Writers, artists and designers, they are married with two children, and spend their time between London and various beaches on the Indian Ocean.

- -

HarperCollins*Entertainment*

An Imprint of HarperCollins*Publishers*

77–85 Fulham Palace Road, Hammersmith, London W6 8JB

www.harpercollins.co.uk

Published by HarperCollins*Entertainment* 2006

2

A catalogue record for this book is available from the British Library

ISBN-10   0 00 723417 1
ISBN-13   978 0 00 723417 2

Set in Bokka

Printed and bound in Italy by Lego SpA

shopping

it's the little voices that tell me to go shopping

Vimrod by LISA SWERLING & RALPH LAZAR

Xmas

christmas is coming. run!

Vimrod by LISA SWERLING & RALPH LAZAR

farting

my farts hospitalise small children

Vimrod by LISA SWERLING & RALPH LAZAR

(watch this space)

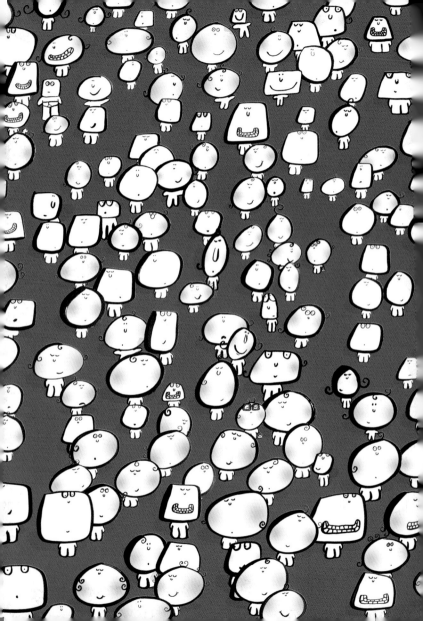